ATTACK VEHICLES
ON LAND

TANKS AND
ARMORED VEHICLES

D0736277

by Craig Boutland

CAPSTONE PRESS
a capstone imprint

Edge Books are published by Capstone Press,
1710 Roe Crest Drive, North Mankato, Minnesota 56003
www.mycapstone.com

Published in 2020 by Capstone Publishing Ltd

Library of Congress Cataloging-in-Publication Data
Cataloging-in-publication information is on file with the Library of Congress.

ISBN: 978-1-5435-7380-0 (library binding)
ISBN: 978-1-5435-7387-9 (eBook PDF)

For Brown Bear Books Ltd:
Editorial Director: Lindsey Lowe
Design Manager: Keith Davis
Children's Publisher: Anne O'Daly
Picture Manager: Sophie Mortimer

Photo Credits
Front Cover: Shutterstock: Andrew Harker.
Interior: Alamy: American Photo Archive, 4-5; Dreamstime: Kamchai Charoenpongchai, 18-19;
iStock: huettenhoelscher, 21t, tramino, 20-21, I M Yeongsik, 18bl; Ministry of Defence UK, 24-2;
Public Domain: Matti Blume, 29t, davric, 22-23, 27r, Gatis Diezins, 29c, Moahmoud Bali (VOA), 7tr, US Airforce/
arcweb.archives.gov, 8, Shutterstock: Andrey Degtyaryov, 29b, Andrew Harker, 1, 8bl, Joseph Sohm, 7tl, Leonard
Zhukovsky, 16-17; US Department of Defense: 10bl, 10-11, 14bl, 28bl, US Airforce, 7b, US Army, 8-9, 22bl, US Army/
TSGT Mike Buylas, 12bl, US Army/Reserve/Master Sgt. Michel Sauret, 14-15, US Army/Sgt. William Tanner, 12-13, US
Marine Corps/Lance Cpl. Juanenrique Owings, 26-27, US Marine Corps/Lance Cpl. Kamran Sadaghiani, 16bl, Staff
Sgt. Dean Wagner, 28tr, Gertrd Zach, 24bl.

Brown Bear Books has made every attempt to contact the copyright holders.
If you have any information please contact licensing@brownbearbooks.co.uk

Printed in China.
1671

TABLE OF CONTENTS

FIGHTING THE WAR ON LAND

The war on terrorism was launched by the United States in 2001. It was a response to the September 11th attacks on the World Trade Center and the Pentagon. Although it is a global war, most military action takes place in Afghanistan, Pakistan, and Iraq.

All branches of the military forces are involved in the war on terrorism. However, as most of the fighting takes place on land, attack vehicles are vital. These vehicles are very heavily armored to resist different types of enemy **projectile**. Battle tanks carry a fearsome array of weapons. Their main guns are accurate over long distances. Attack vehicles also have machine guns and rapid firing cannon. Sometimes these weapons are fired directly by the crew. At other times, weapons are fired using Remote Controlled Weapons Systems (RCWS).

projectile—an object, such as a bullet or missile, that is thrown or shot through the air with intent to cause damage

A Bradley M3A3 Infantry Fighting Vehicle on a mission in Iraq.

TIMELINE OF THE WAR ON TERRORISM

September 2001

Terrorists from a group called al-Qaeda, led by Osama bin Laden, capture four U.S. commercial airliners. Two of the airplanes are flown into the twin towers of the World Trade Center in New York City. The Pentagon in Washington, D.C. is also attacked. The fourth plane crash lands in Pennsylvania. In total, 2,996 people die.

February 2006

Al-Qaeda bombs the Shia al-Askari Mosque in Iraq. This is part of widespread violence between Sunni and Shia Muslims in Iraq. Tens of thousands of people die.

 2001　　 **2003**　　 **2006**　　**2011**

October–November 2001

U.S. forces and their **coalition allies** invade Afghanistan, where al-Qaeda was based. Afghanistan is run by the Taliban, an extreme Islamic political group. Coalition forces quickly overrun the country. They capture the capital, Kabul, in November. The Taliban go into hiding and continue the war.

March–December 2003

U.S. and coalition forces invade Iraq. They capture the capital, Baghdad, in April. In December, Iraqi president Saddam Hussein is captured. Islamic extremists and other groups fight on against the coalition forces.

May 2011

A U.S. Navy SEAL team locates and kills Osama bin Laden in Pakistan, where he had been in hiding.

December 2014
U.S. President Barack Obama announces the end of the U.S. combat role in Afghanistan. Afghan government forces take over all combat duties as the war against the forces of the Taliban continues.

January 2015
ISIS (a terrorist group sometimes called Islamic State) splits away from al-Qaeda. ISIS takes control of the city of Fallujah in Iraq.

October 2017
ISIS loses control of Raqqa, its last major stronghold in Iraq. It has also been forced to withdraw from major towns in Syria. From October 2014 to 2017, U.S. forces launched more than 20,000 air strikes against ISIS in Iraq and Syria.

2014   **2015**   **2017**   **2018**

April 2014
The Boko Haram Islamic extremist group in Nigeria kidnaps 276 female school students. In 2018, 112 of them were still missing.

December 2015
ISIS takes control of large areas of Iraq and Syria. It enforces strict Islamic laws that set out how Muslims should lead their lives. "Operation Inherent Resolve" is launched against ISIS by U.S. attack aircraft.

June 2018
The Afghan government and the Taliban announce a ceasefire for the Eid holiday that ends Ramadan.

coalition allies—members of a group of people or countries working together toward a common goal

M1A1 ABRAMS MBT

The Abrams M1A1 is a main battle tank (MBT). It **spearheaded** the U.S. invasion of Iraq to overthrow the government of president Saddam Hussein in 2003. He was suspected of helping the terrorist group, al-Qaeda.

IN ACTION

On patrol, ammunition is carried in a separate box. If the tank is hit by enemy fire, the crew area is protected from exploding ammunition.

MAIN WEAPON is the 120mm gun. It fires different types of shells, depending on the target.

TOP-MOUNTED MACHINE GUN can be remote-controlled by the commander in the tank.

LOADED WEIGHT: 68.5 tons (62 metric tons)

LENGTH: (including gun) 32 feet (10 meters)

OFF-ROAD SPEED: 30 miles (48 kilometers) per hour

CREW: four

MAIN WEAPONS: 120mm gun, 12.7mm machine gun, 7.62mm machine guns

TRACKS are partly protected by the tank's side armor.

spearhead—to lead the attack in a campaign or military operation

M3A3 BRADLEY IFV

The M3A3 Infantry Fighting Vehicle (IFV) plays a significant support role. It carries a wide range of weapons. Between 2003 and 2008 it was used to patrol cities and towns in Iraq.

IN ACTION

The M3A3 is designed for observation and patrol. It carries extra weaponry and two infantrymen, who act as scouts in war zones.

SMOKE GRENADES can be launched from the turret to help conceal the Bradley in action.

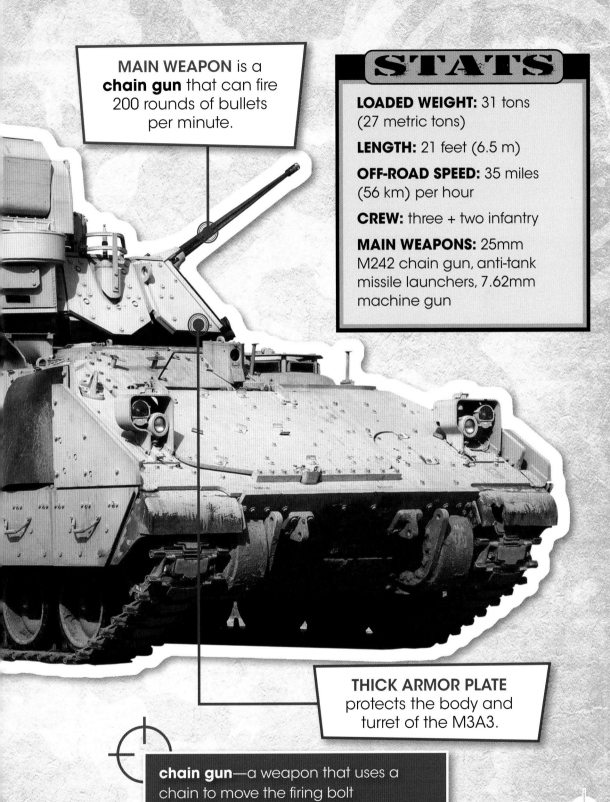

MAIN WEAPON is a **chain gun** that can fire 200 rounds of bullets per minute.

THICK ARMOR PLATE protects the body and turret of the M3A3.

chain gun—a weapon that uses a chain to move the firing bolt

STRYKER

Strykers are a family of eight-wheeled combat vehicles. Strykers entered service with the U.S. Army in 2003. Since then, Strykers have been in service in the war on terrorism in Afghanistan and Iraq.

IN ACTION

Strykers are able to move fast in cities or open **terrain**. The people carrier transports infantry quickly to battlefield positions. The mobile gun system (MGS) vehicle provides fire support for infantry in battle.

EIGHT WHEELS give the Stryker speed and mobility.

MOBILE GUN SYSTEM in the turret is fitted with an autoloader. This means the crew can fire the guns from inside the vehicle.

ARMOR can be added to the sides of the vehicle to protect it against enemy fire.

terrain—the surface features of an area of land

M113A3 APC

The M113 is a U.S. Army armored personnel carrier (APC). It transports infantry into battle. The M113 was developed to be light enough to transport into war zones by airplane. M113s are used worldwide.

IN ACTION

The M113 can carry 11 infantry alongside the crew. The troop compartment is fully enclosed with high quality aluminum armor. This is light, but very strong.

THICK ALUMINUM ARMOR gives the same high levels of protection as steel armor.

ANTI-TANK MISSILES can be fitted alongside the main machine gun.

STATS

LOADED WEIGHT: 14 tons (12.5 metric tons)

LENGTH: 16 feet (5 m)

TOP SPEED: 42 miles (67 km) per hour

CREW: two + 11 passengers

MAIN WEAPON: M2 Browning machine gun, plus anti-tank missiles (optional)

FLAPS on the **caterpillar tracks** act like oars to propel the vehicle through water.

caterpillar tracks—a belt of metal plates that pass around the wheels of a vehicle to help it move across rough terrain

LAV-25

The LAV-25 (Light Armored Vehicle), is eight-wheeled, **amphibious**, and armored. It can transport six U.S. Marines, as well as the crew. The vehicle was used in Afghanistan in 2001, and in the invasion of Iraq in 2003.

A STREAMLINED HULL is designed to help the vehicle cross streams, rivers, and inland waterways.

IN ACTION

The LAV-25 has a fully rotational gun turret. It can swing around 360 degrees. One of the machine guns is mounted alongside the main chain gun.

FULL HULL AND TURRET ARMOR protects the vehicle from machine gun and shell fire.

LOADED WEIGHT: 15 tons (13 metric tons)

LENGTH: 21 feet (6.5 m)

TOP SPEED: 62 miles (100 km) per hour

CREW: three crew and six passengers

MAIN WEAPONS: 25mm chain gun, 7.62mm machine guns

THE REAR DOORS open for Marines to enter and leave the vehicle.

amphibious—a vehicle that can operate on land or in the sea

ASSAULT AMPHIBIOUS VEHICLE AAVP7A1

The AAVP7A1 has two roles. It can transfer up to 25 U.S. Marines in full combat gear from **assault ships** to the shore. Once on land, it becomes a transport vehicle.

VESSEL-SHAPED HULL allows the vehicle to travel through 10 foot (3 m) waves.

IN ACTION

The AAVP7A1 has excellent mobility over all terrains. It can reach a top speed of 45 miles (72 km) per hour on land.

GUN TURRET
can turn through
360 degrees
at a speed
of 45 degrees
per second.

STATS

LOADED WEIGHT: 23 tons
(20 metric tons)

LENGTH: 26 feet (8 m)

TOP SPEED: 8 miles (13 km)
per hour in water

CREW: three crew and up to 25
passengers

MAIN WEAPONS: 40 mm grenade
launcher, .50 machine gun

718

ALUMINUM HULL
protects the crew from
small arms fire.

assault ship—an ocean-going troopship used
to transport troops to enemy territory

LEOPARD 2A5

The Leopard is a main battle tank (MBT). It is heavy and has powerful weapons. The Turkish Army used Leopards against ISIS terrorists in Syria in 2017.

STATS

LOADED WEIGHT: 69 tons (61 metric tons)

LENGTH INCLUDING GUN: 33 feet (10 m)

TOP SPEED: 45 miles (72 km) per hour

CREW: four

MAIN WEAPONS: 120mm smoothbore gun, .50 machine gun, coaxial 7.62mm machine guns

MAIN GUN fires high-explosive anti-tank shells and armor-piercing cartridges.

ARMOR protection is **multi-layered** for strength and is angled to help deflect bullets.

In 2008, Leopard 2A5 tanks were used in Helmand Province, Afghanistan. They were effective against the Taliban. The tanks were mainly used as gunfire support for infantry operations.

THE CREW uses computerized systems to aim and fire the main gun.

multi-layered—armor built from layers of different materials, such as ceramics, titanium, and steel

WARRIOR

The Warrior is a British tracked armored vehicle. Its job is to carry soldiers into battle and provide support to the main battle tanks. Warriors have been in action against terrorism in all conflicts since 2002.

IN ACTION

The Warrior carries up to 7 fully-equipped soldiers. The vehicles were important in the conflict in Afghanistan (2002–2014), and supported Britain's main battle tanks in the Iraq War (2003–2011).

36 KG 44

STRENGTHENED ARMOR belly plates underneath protect against enemy roadside **IEDs**.

THE TURRET contains hi-tech thermal imaging equipment for night operations.

STATS

LOADED WEIGHT: 26.5 tons (24 metric tons)

LENGTH: 20 feet (6.3 m)

OFF-ROAD SPEED: 46 miles (75 km) per hour

CREW: three + seven soldiers

MAIN WEAPONS: 30mm cannon, 7.62mm chain gun, 7.62mm machine gun

SOLDIERS enter the Warrior by the single rear door.

IED—stands for improvised explosive device; IEDs are homemade bombs often made with material not usually found in bombs

CHALLENGER 2

The British Challenger 2 main battle tank has played an important role in Iraq. Roadside bombs and bombs set off by individuals carrying or wearing them have changed the nature of modern warfare. Challenger is equipped to protect the crew.

SIDE ARMOR of the Challenger 2 is multi-layered and twice as strong as the armor on older tanks.

IN ACTION

Challenger 2 was introduced in 1998. The body was higher off the ground to lessen the impact of bomb blasts. The crew have special seats protected by iron plates.

LOADED WEIGHT: 82.7 tons (75 metric tons)

LENGTH INCLUDING GUN: 44 feet (13.5 m)

TOP SPEED: 37 miles (59 km) per hour

CREW: four

MAIN WEAPONS: 120mm rifled gun, 7.62mm chain gun, 7.62mm machine gun

A GROOVED GUN BARREL spins the shell as it flies through the air. This makes it fly more accurately toward its target.

CHALLENGERS are extremely strong. One Challenger in Iraq was hit by 70 **RPGs** but survived.

RPG—shoulder-fired, anti-tank weapons; stands for rocket propelled grenade

AMX-10RC

The French-made AMX-10RC is a powerful weapon against other armored vehicles, buildings, and other targets. It has been used extensively in the war in Afghanistan, and against Islamic **extremists** in Mali.

STATS

LOADED WEIGHT: 17 tons (15 metric tons)

LENGTH INCLUDING GUN: 30 feet (9 m)

OFF-ROAD SPEED: 24 miles (40 km) per hour

CREW: four

MAIN WEAPONS: 105mm main gun, coaxial 7.62mm machine gun, 2.7mm machine gun

CENTRAL TIRE PRESSURE SYSTEM adjusts the tire pressures for different types of terrain, such as sand, mud, or snow.

FIRE SUPPORT for main battle tanks is the primary role of the AMX-10RC. It accompanies them into action.

IN ACTION

The AMX-10RC fires four types of ammunition. Two are for destroying armored vehicles. Another is for use against enemy soldiers. The fourth is a smoke grenade, for protection.

SUSPENSION is adjustable. The AMX body can be raised up to 2 feet (0.7 m) above ground level.

extremist—a person who holds extreme religious or political views

OTHER TANKS AND ARMORED VEHICLES

Many different types of tanks and land vehicles are needed to meet the challenges of terrorism. Armor protection is important. No one knows where the next bomb will come from.

AMX-30B2 MBT

This amphibious armored car was developed for the Vietnam War (1955–1975), where it operated in jungle terrain. It was later used in operations against ISIS terrorist groups in the Philippines.

M706 Cadillac Gage Commando

The AMX-30B2 MBT is a lightly armored French main battle tank. It relies on speed, rather than heavy armor, for protection. The tank played a major part in the Gulf War (1990–1991) against Iraq.

This is a German light armored patrol vehicle. It has a top speed of 59 miles (95 km) per hour. The first Enoks delivered in 2008 were used by German special forces. They are also used as armed airport security patrols against terrorist threats.

CVRs

The CVR stands for Combat Vehicle Reconnaissance. These armored vehicles are used by armies worldwide. Since 2001, they have been used extensively in the conflicts in Afghanistan, Iran, and Iraq.

T-90

The Russian T-90 is a main battle tank. In 2015, 30 T-90s were sent to Syria in support of president Bashar al-Assad's government. The tank is protected by Kontakt-5 **explosive-reactive armor**.

explosive-reactive armor—armor that explodes outward when hit, rather than inward, to minimize interior damage

GLOSSARY

amphibious (am-FI-bee-uhs)—a vehicle that can operate on land or in the sea

assault ship (ah-SAWLT SHIP)—an ocean-going troopship used to transport troops to enemy territory

caterpillar tracks (KA-tur-pil-luhr TRAKS)—a belt of metal plates that pass around the wheels of a vehicle to help it move across rough terrain

chain gun (CHAYNE GUN)—a weapon that uses a chain to move the bolt

coalition allies (koh-uh-LISH-uhn AL-eyes)—members of a group of people or countries working together toward a common goal

explosive-reactive armor (ex-PLOH-siv ree-AK-tiv AR-muhr)—armor that explodes outward when hit, rather than inward, to minimize interior damage

extremist (ek-STREEM-ist)—a person who holds extreme religious or political views

IED (EYE-ee-dee)—stands for improvised explosive device; IEDs are homemade bombs often made with material not usually found in bombs

multi-layered (muhl-tee-LAY-urd)—armor built from layers of different materials, such as ceramics, titanium, and steel

projectile (pruh-JEK-tuhl)—an object, such as a bullet or missile, that is thrown or shot through the air with intent to cause damage

RPG (ar-pee-GEE)—stands for rocket propelled grenade. These are shoulder-fired, anti-tank weapons.

spearhead (SPEER-hed)—to lead the attack on a campaign or military operation

terrain (tuh-RAYN)—the surface features of an area of land

READ MORE

Hunt, Jilly. *The Fight Against War and Terrorism.*
Beyond the Headlines! Chicago: Capstone Press, 2018

Levete, Sarah. *The Army.* Military Defend and Protect.
New York: Gareth Stevens Publishing, 2016

Nagelhout, Ryan. *Tanks.* Mighty Military Machines.
New York: Gareth Stevens Publishing, 2015

Summers, Elizabeth. *Weapons and Vehicles of the Iraq War.*
Tools of War. North Mankato, MN: Capstone Press, 2016

INTERNET SITES

Modern Tanks
https://www.militaryfactory.com/armor/modern-tanks.asp

Tanks and Fighting Vehicles
https://www.goarmy.com/about/army-vehicles-and-equipment/
tanks-and-fighting-vehicles.html

**The U.S. Army's Latest Armored Vehicle Could Have a Game
Changing Upgrade**
https://nationalinterest.org/blog/the-buzz/the-us-armys-latest-
armored-vehicle-could-have-game-changing-23016

What is the Role of Tanks in Warfare Today?
https://aoav.org.uk/2013/what-is-the-role-of-tanks-in-warfare-today/

INDEX